WRITING THERAPY

Monique Kwachou

Langaa Research & Publishing CIG
Mankon, Bamenda

Publisher:

Langaa RPCIG
Langaa Research & Publishing Common Initiative Group
P.O. Box 902 Mankon
Bamenda
North West Region
Cameroon
Langaagrp@gmail.com
www.langaa-rpcig.net

Distributed outside N. America by African Books Collective
orders@africanbookscollective.com
www.africanbookcollective.com

Distributed in N. America by Michigan State University Press
msupress@msu.edu
www.msupress.msu.edu

ISBN: 978-9956-578-06-1

Dedication

This collection is dedicated to;

God for blessing me with the talent to express myself,

To all the great ladies in my life:

My mother's; Ma Ess, Ms. Pamela Kouchou, Ms.

Maria Fokwa, Ms. Kometa M.C, Ma Cheng, & Mami

Fokam

My sisters; K. Christy, Mbeh Njah, N. Sandrine, N.

Grace, & Mimi

For knowing me and still loving me!

Table of Content

Part Three: Writings of the Spirit. 37

Part One

I'M WRITING

I'm writing for my freedom
I'm writing for my dreams
I'm writing this here poem
For my heart expresses the need!

I'm singing for my future
For the vision that I see
I'm singing of my heart's desire,
For the reason that I live.

I'm living for tomorrow,
And for a better day!
When dreams shall be reality
And joy shall move sorrow away.

I'm hoping in a miracle,
Believing in a wish,
Praying God blesses me soon
And his purpose in my life fulfill!

THE COURAGE TO LIVE

It takes courage to See…
What lies before your eyes
Rather than ignore
the harsh realities of our time.

It takes courage to Dream…
And in those dreams believe,
To hope in a future
That has no guarantee.

It takes courage to Love…
And believe you can be loved
To trust another with your heart,
To share your best and your worst.

It takes courage to Be…
Who you are, no more no less
No product of Society,
But a heretic in itself!

I t takes courage to Believe…
In others, in yourself
Above all to believe
There's a God who truly cares!
It Takes Courage to LIVE!!!

SPEAK!

Speak now so you may speak again!
If I laugh too much…
It's because I have cried too much
And I prefer the laughter better.

Speak now so you may speak again!
If I feel too deep…
It's because I know the pain inflicted by the stoic
And I would prefer even pain to emotional void.

Speak now so you may speak again!
If I trust too much…
It's because I know destructiveness of distrust,
And the power of trust on another's esteem.

Speak now so you may speak again!
If I keep silent…
It's because I have learnt that; actions speak louder
And I await the right time to act.

Speak now so you may speak again!
If I speak now…
It's because I've been pushed to the wall,
And I would speak my mind once and for all.

IN OUR SILENCE

(An ode to Cameroon)

In our silence… we are robbed!
Of our rights, of our might!
And forced to take our God-given birthright
As man given privilege!

In our silence… we are abused
Insulted, oppressed and misused
By the very leaders
Who by franchise we choose!

In our silence… we deny
Ourselves, children and nation alike
Prosperity, what should be
We remain surviving while others live!

In our silence… we kill our dreams
And destroy our hope, already so frail
Under the cover of false peace, the truth is
We are weak and fear to fail!

In our silence… we die
For all but spitting in a politicians eye!
Of hunger, disease in a land of milk and honey!
And dying, our silence goes on!

In our silence… we stop
Haven reached the end of our rope,

Haven lost all our hope
We die of the inability to cope!

TODAY

Today is all we have
No matter how hard for tomorrow we strive
The time shall never fly
Unless good days are nigh!

Yesterday is forever gone,
Blissful ignorance, innocence forgone
Past mistakes often regretted much,
Yet the lessons we ought to have learnt often forgot.

Of tomorrow we can never tell,
Only hope in our hearts shall dwell
And solely faith can enable us live…
In a world that's but a few steps up from hell.

Yes, today is all we have, live it well!
Fervent prayer for tomorrow, appreciation for yesterday
Neither rushing forward nor looking back;
But living in the moment like it's all we have!

WORD POWER

There is power in the word,
Power in the written word
To express what the eyes can't say
Or what worries the mind day by day
To move someone to tears,
To record history throughout the years

There is power in a word,
Power in the spoken word
The speech that fuels the masses to rise,
Or that song that brings tears to your eyes.
Herein lays the power to console, inspire and oppress
The spoken word never fails to express!

There is power in the word,
Power in the silent word.
Like the words which were left unsaid
For which a needy heart yearns,
Or the words which are suppressed, locked down deep
While the patriot his courage seeks.

Be it the sentence in a speech,
The poets' stanza or song lyrics,
There is power in the word!
Expressing, destroying, inspiring and never failing
But greatest is the power of God's Word
The life saving, ever-loving, ever-living Word of God!

HOMELESS

Homeless, in a furnished prison
Ignored yet catered for
Feelings of inadequacy reign in me
Yearning for attention I'll never receive
I'm blessed and cursed it seems.

Homeless, sitting in a crowded room, unbelonging and
odd
Yearning for a kindred spirit
Who will with me life's road trod,
But knowing that person I'll never meet.

Homeless, feeling like a fish on land and so tired of it!
Dreaming of the ocean blue
Not an aquarium of luxury
Accused of ingratitude, and fearing it's true.

Homeless, rebelling in a fit of passion
Following my heart… left the catered prison behind
Now not only homeless I stand, but houseless as well.

SHAPES OF FEAR

Square like the door shut in your face,
Like the cell which is the patriots resting place
Like a letter of rejection
Square like the coffin of a small boy.

Round like addictive pills
Like the hole of a snake pit
Like the face of a crying child
Round like the barrel of a gun pointed toward
you at night

But still shapes are our greatest fears,
Like the fear of disappointment
Fear that we would fail
Fear that our belief is in vain!

Varied in shape and size are our fears
Yet what cripples us most
Is the fear of the unknown?
Conquer the fear and live free on your own!

PENSIVE

We walk the road of life often blind,
Not for lack of sight, but for loss of mind
And many a time, we stumble and fall.
Great are they who find the courage to rise yet again and
stand tall!

To linger on the past ...
Is to dim the light of the present,
And create clouds of future gloom
And hinder the forgetting even after haven forgiven

In the walk of life be pensive knowing
Age marks nothing but the multitude of life's
experiences weathered
And that we see things better
When we view failure as simply another chance to do
better

A FALLEN PEOPLE

Black is the color of our skin
But darker yet our inner beings
For failure to see the light, to own up to our flaws
We remain blight.
From the false preachers to the political yes men
Its blind leading blind,
And into the crater-like pot holes we all fall
And the power-drunk sots would dare to talk of
communalism!
We are fallen, crippled at that!
By disunity, short-sight,
Hopelessness
Haven been at the bottom for so long
We forget to struggle to rise again
We make our homes in the crater –like pot holes
Only our grumbling betraying our facade of contentment
Yes we are the fallen people
Dark without and within
Because we refuse learn from history's lesson
But repeat it again and again
No longer fighting to live but content to survive
We no longer strive to better what is
And our misery visible only in our sighs
Yes nations of the fallen are we!

SUPERWOMAN

Super woman…
Bearing the future in her womb
Nurturing generations with her love
Her dreams buried in her heart
For a future of which she has no part

Superwoman…
Cooking by the fireside
Feeding a multitude twice her size
Tilling, Bent from dawn to twilight
Oh! Her strength, What a sight!

Super woman…
Her neglected mind ever working still
Not nurtured by books but with skill
Experience the only tutor she receives,
Barely surviving, how can she live?

Superwoman…
If actions would speak louder than words
Her deeds would fairly scream
For silent though she has been
Her actions hold the world at its seams

Superwoman…
Haven been silent so long,
And in that silence, belittled, abused, scorned
Finally daring to speak her mind
She fights for a better day for her kind!

A WOMAN'S WORTH

A woman's worth is often lost
in her kitchen pot,
And from her pot to the mouths of men
who appreciate it not

A woman's worth is only seen
in her husband's conceited gait,
For none would pay any mind
To the work she does all day!

A woman's worth is heralded
By the lusty cries of a male child
After all, what is a girl?
A minion, someone's future wife

A woman's worth is a shadow, is it not?
Of her husband's considerable lack thereof
But then a Diamond in the dirt…
Does not make it less a diamond, thank God!

BLACK WOMAN

I am woman
And she is me,
I shall be true
to my identity
I m pretty, no more no less
For beauty is left
for those who see to decree!

I am alive!
mind body and soul,
I feel; ache, pain and need,
I cry, laugh, and dream
Constantly wonder why
Never rein my emotions,
but leave them free to fly

I am black,
African, the better minority
Never ashamed, but proud to be
Of a color that has such history
Not always privileged but ever-striving
Born of passion, blessed with spirit
This keeps a people light despite the dark

I am loved,
Lovable, loving
Dream-filled, aspiring
Blessed by divinity,

16

Daughter of a king
Not a mere ruler,
But the almighty creator!

THE PROBLEM WITH DREAMING

The problem with dreaming,
Is that you begin believing,
Believing, until your cut short,
Eventually by reality

And believing begets wishing
Wishing built on the uncertainty of hope
And hope often frail seems lacking
As a source of strength to cope

And this wishing begets yearning
Yearning like a fire burning,
Consuming your thoughts by day
And at night more dreams fueling

And so the dreaming returns
A product of wishes and wants
The greatest problem being that dawn must break
And the dreamer awake!

HOUR GLASS

At dawn, at peace, we languish, care free and at ease
Yet thankless for this state, oblivious to the trials ahead
Ungrateful for the peace, unaware of that such is luxury
Then come then noon with its pressures and passions,
And restlessness replaces and we are no longer at ease
Slowly cares and worries fill our minds
And under their weight we bend
To breaking point
Innocence destroyed
Broken
We are broken by life!
Past the heat and passion of noon
And post-breakage, a cool twilight indeed
With memories of the noon, of foolishness thereof
And lessons learnable only by experience now taught
With life's pressures no longer as important as before
Patience now an achievement, the speed of life now slow
Allowing the mind emerge profound, behold a sage is
born
And the peace of dawn returns, but now the luxury
recognized as such!

AFRICA

"What do you see when you look at me?" asked mother
Africa
"I see beautiful landscapes nature at its purest,
Magnificent mountains like rooftops
Alongside, drought ravaged lands,
And desserts were only the dead can live!"

"I see a multitude of colors in every fabric sown
Yet a people ashamed of the color their skin shows
I see the proud, women like Queen Nzinga of old
And I see those robed with shame,
Struggling to bleach their black away!"

"What to do you hear when you listen to me?" Asked
mama Africa
"I hear a variety of tongues and the disunity I them,
I hear so called leaders lip singing to the tune of the west
For fear (or is it unwillingness) to use the voice
With which they were blessed!"

"I hear the cries of children who have no food to eat
And the false words of pot-bellied politicians
With Italian leather shoes on their feet
I hear the screams of those who would stand against the
rape of the land
And the contrasting silence when they are caught"

"What do you feel when you think of me?" asked
mother Africa
"I feel the frustration of the people who get reports
Of fertile soils, mineral riches but still die in poverty!
I feel the discomfort of the grumblers
Who grumble yet refuse to act for change!"

"I feel the hopelessness of the youth
As they ponder on their vice-ridden nations
I feel the pain of the aged at thinking their fought
colonialism in vain
I feel the desire of the continent to fulfill its potential,
Yet the sadness of knowing it may never be! "

"Yes!" says Mama Africa,
"You know me well, my child!
Both blessed and cursed, here I lie
Waiting for they who would love the whole above
themselves
To help me raise my head my head up high!"

MYSREALISM

Writing in disquiet not without but within
Perplexed and bewildered by life's constant mazing
Like children weaned on fairytales,
We fight a war each day:
What we dream against what we see,
Our beliefs versus reality
Trying to reconcile what we imagine
With what we truly live
Fact versus reality it seems

Our greatest battle then is with ourselves,
Do we continue with our dreams?
Do we pass on the "once upon a times"?
And hope "happily ever after" shall be the end?
Do we feed the fairytales to our young again
Knowing that the truth is by far different

Neither optimism nor pessimism shall do you see
And yet realism is closer to the latter negative scene
At least with our fairytales we give spread a little light
To help young ones see when reality seems blight
The tales might be false and far from the truth,
But life has a better chance
When you start it with hope

Part Two

WRITINGS OF MY HEART

These are the writings of my heart
The speeches of my soul
The thoughts I try to express
While in my mind they roll

These are the secrets of my dreams
Revealed by my pen
The thoughts on which I ponder
As I lay in bed

These are the words of my emotions
Expressed in stanza form,
The burdens of my heart and mind
Over which my soul is torn

These are the dictates of my spirit
Made out into rhyme
The cares and worries that move me
Exposed to be solved by time.

And so the writings of my heart
I on this sheet record
To share a piece of me
With one and all!

MY ANGEL

My angel doesn't flow in a gown of white,
She wears Armani to work and gets runs in her tights
But she proves she's angelic
When she comes home to me at night
My angel is my wife.

My angel is not present for every Sunday sermon
But she instilled in me the values I based my life on
She's an angel as she emits love by weight in tons
And in my life she has been a guiding force,
My angel is my mom.

My angel isn't gentle in his way of life
But he tries to the right thing at all times
I should know as I'm his wife
He gave me a reason to live when no one seemed to
care,
My angel is the father of my child.

My angel can't be trusted when it comes to whites,
He's barely three feet tall when we talk of height
His virtues are humility, innocence and purity of heart
Into my life he shines the brightest light,
My angel is my child.

ONLY YOU

More than words of comfort
More than any gifts
Nothing else will keep me tranquil
My heart needs what only you can give

Only you can make me smile
When there seems no reason to
Or lighten my spirit
When the burden of cares cause my chest to swell

Only you can understand
What I am yet to say,
And know sometimes it's a shove and not a hug
I need to keep crises at bay

Only you can make me feel
Invincible, lovely, free
Only you my heart's desire
Can give me the loving that I need

MY LOVE

I waiting for my love
For the one who'll sweep me off my feet
One who will speak to me with fervor
One who will make me laugh and weep

I'm dreaming of my love
No fantasy of a charming prince,
But a vision of a steady partner
Walk the paths of life with.

I'm wishing for my love
He who God made just for me
Who will love me as I am
Yet help me be a better me

And when I find my love
The one who will share my desire,
I'll give my thanks to God
And of loving him I shall never tire!

NEED

Feel my need
The need that grows within
And controls my every dream
Feel my need
That keeps my heart burning
And my soul forever yearning
Feel my need
The need to give you all I am
And receive naught in turn but the comfort of your arms
Feel my need
To share with you my soul and love you as we grow old
Satisfy my need
To be yours as the years unfold.

THE CONTRACT

Marriage…
Two

Becoming

One

Lovingly

Entwined
Divinely
Legalized
Believing in
Each other

And in belief

Living,

Forming an

Ageless Union

MUSINGS AT DAWN

Is there a hospital for my broken heart?
Is there a cure for its ache?
Is there a soul that feels the way I do
Every morning I awake?

Is there a poem which can my feelings describe?
Or a song for the wailings of my heart?
Is there any glue to hold my being together?
As my spirit falls apart.

Is there a state as morose as loneliness?
Or any loss as painful as death?
Are there any words more aching?
Than those that were yet to be said.

And as I write I wonder
Is there any hope to be had?
For a day which would begin
With such musing at dawn

TO BE LONELY

To be lonely
Is to cry alone…
For lack of a shoulder you can lean on
It means holding on to your dreams
For want of a partner to share it with

To be lonely
Is to sleep at night dreaming of a loved one's embrace
Then waking in the morning with a chill at your breast
It's to yearn to the point of tears
And pray for nothing else

To be lonely
is to search for a like mind
In an ocean of opposites
It's to suppress your personality
For fear of social animosity

To be lonely
Is to create your own world
Where you depend on you alone
To choose not to trust,
For fear of disappointment

To be lonely
Is to lay on the road alone when you fall
For there's no helping hand to lift you

To be lonely is not to be alone,
It's to be without!

DREAMING OF YOU

My dreams are many and they are few
But all are filled with you!
My once heavy heart is now made light
For your presence in my life
I dream of long days filled with our laughter,
And longer nights sharing our warmth
I dream of a future with the sole guarantee
Of your unconditional love.
I dream of a kindred spirit,
To laugh with and to cry,
A friend and a lover
I dream of loving you forever!

BROKEN

The ache in your chest, that you cannot explain,
The void that somehow feels heavy.
That emptiness that will not be assuaged,
And the burden of unfulfillment
… That's a broken heart.

The weakness you feel in simply living
The fatigue from trying so hard in vain
That nagging self doubt,
And absence of willpower to fight again
… That is a broken spirit

The loss of hope,
And they joy and faith with which it comes
That feeling of losing
What was never truly yours
…That's a broken dream

That feeling of inadequacy,
That makes you forget your worth
And eats at you inside
Till your alive and yet a corpse
…That's a broken life!

We live in a broken world

Part Three

THE MUSE

Reactivating my stagnant blood
Reviving my senses to this world
The spirit of the omnipresent God
Awakening my soul within me
My spirit moved, the words now flow
Uninhibited, telling what my heart knows
The muse, my gift
Seeing with my hearts eye
Feeling with the spirit
Thinking of how another's mind may perceive
The muse: empathy
God given.

THE WORD

When all around my life's in shambles,
The Word seems like nothing but ramblings
When in my soul I feel a riot,
The Word and all its lessons are void

And when my mind hurts with craving,
To understand a life so hazy
The Word is seemingly vague,
And life nothing but a plague

Then as time would passes by
I see my worries suddenly fly
Hurled away by that very Word
Which my mind had ignored

And so I know all in all
There's a book on which I can always call
No matter how the world may lie,
There is power in the Word none can deny

The Word of God is alive!

WITHOUT A DOUBT

Without a doubt I know…
That life is not an easy road
Without a doubt I know...
That man is but an ocean drifted boat

I am aware …
That the chances are slim
And hope as frail as an infant's health
And tomorrow as uncertain as to what may be

Even ever conscious of…
The pains that strike our hearts
Disappointments that callous our spirits
And destroy our trust in life

Ever alert of …
The emotions battling within
The weakness of human will
And the readiness to sin
Yet without A doubt I know…
That I am divinely loved
Preciously redeemed
By he who shed his blood

And even more certain…
That my cares shall be overcome
For by my side stands an omnipotent God
And he loves me as I am, without a doubt!

MY INSPIRATION
(Dedicated to my father at heart)

You're the one who gave me courage,
The one who gave me hope
The one who helped me onward
Up the steep, steep slope

You're the one who said "of course you can"
When no one else did same
The one who lent a helping hand
By giving me your faith

You're the one who cared to listen
While I dreamt aloud
The only one who believed in my ability
To reach beyond the clouds

You're the one I fear to let down
Even just a fraction
For in my life, you have been
My one true inspiration!

MOTHER

Nine months in your womb I spent
And thereafter through labor you wept,
Tears of pain and joy alike
You dreamt of me through that first night,
My mother

Day by day on your breast I fed
While you smiled and patted my head
My first steps may have been to the moon
For as you recounted it you seemed to swoon
My mother

At the least sign of illness, you cried
Your love for me shining in your eyes
The one who for me always had time to lend
Who could scold and still be my best friend
My mother

She who remained my role model till dying day,
Motivated me in every way
And who is now gone taking along a part of my core
And whom I now wish I had treasured more!
My mother

A FRIEND

A friend is a shoulder that never grows weak
No matter how many times it's leaned on
A friend is a diary that understands
Even what is left unwritten
A friend is a partner in every fall,
And the one who applauds the loudest when victory calls

friends are many but Friends are few
For it's a blessing to find a friend who is true
Who will slap your hands
As much as kiss your cheek
With whom you can always talk
And be sure they will just listen.

Someone to trust
When you don't trust yourself,
Who knows you in and out
And still loves you then
Who takes you as you are
Yet challenges you to be better

A friend is that ray of light
That makes the diamond in you shine
Not only one who is there to love us
But one who needs our love just as much
A gift for all to have if they would
A Friend is treasure true!

WHAT HOPE MEANS TO ME

A little ray of sunshine
Filtering through the cracks
of the cage where the captive sits

A beam as strong as iron
Though it wavers in the wind
Tremulous yet unbreaking

That feeling in your heart
Lifting you up to try again
Springing within you the strength to cope

That rhythm in your heart
Making you sing
Even when your voice is lost!

The foundation of our every dream
The essence of our very being
Yes! That's what Hope means to me.